MW00887667

BOUNCING BACK TO ME:

Overcoming Jealousy, Depression and More

Chimeko Hodge,

Thank you for the support!
God Bless ♡
— Jyrah Wal—

BOUNCING BACK TO ME:

Overcoming Jealousy, Depression and More

Tyrah M. Walker

Bouncing Back to Me

FIRST EDITION

Library of Congress Cataloging-in-Publication Data has been applied for.

ISBN-13: 978-1721226825
ISBN-10: 1721226826
Library of Congress Control Number
Create Space Independent Publishing Platform
North Charleston. South Carolina

Cover photography design by DomWarpedVision
Book interior design by Amikco N. Marolt @
TheMeCo@gmail.com.

Editing by Amikco N. Marolt and Ninon Rhome

Bouncing Back to Me

This book is dedicated to the men and women who have lost themselves in the midst of adversity. This is a reminder to you that God will always be there for you. All you have to do is call on Him. This book is also dedicated to the people who know they have callings over their life but may need that extra push. This book is for the people who are in toxic relationships and don't know how to get out. Know that you can and you will bounce back from all your circumstances with the help of Jesus Christ.

Love, *Tyrah*

Table of Contents

Prelude

I sat crying as I waited for Tamara to come home. I sat in my car pouring out tears just waiting for Tamara to come home from work. I had sent her a text twenty minutes earlier, begging her to hurry up and rescue me.

"Tamara I am outside of your house. I need you!" the message said.

Indeed, I needed her. At that moment, I really needed my sister. I just sat there crying outside of her home. I didn't have anywhere else to go and I had no one to talk to. I felt that God didn't want to hear me.

How did I get to this point? Did I miss the signs? He didn't want me. He wanted someone else. I saw the pictures. God, every time I saw pictures of the two of them, I broke a little more inside. Why did I let this happen? Is this what depression felt like? Hurry up Tamara! Hurry up and get off from work!

I knew I shouldn't have been crying, but it didn't matter. I knew that I was better than this, but it was too late. He loved me though…or at least I thought he loved me. Maybe he wasn't in his right mind. Well why am I crying so hard? We never had sex so why am I crying as if we did? I'm a virgin so it doesn't make sense that I'm crying like this.

The two of them! I could only think of the two of them and the idea of them being together. That's what it was. That was the trigger. Where is my sister? Tamara hurry up and get home, now!

Bouncing Back to Me

Alone in the car, I had tears pouring down my face, while looking at their photo. Then a few minutes later, she finally pulled up.

She said, "Morris let me call you back. Tyrah is in her car crying."

Tamara opens my car door. She tries to pull me out. I just can't stop crying. It's hot outside. When did it get so hot outside?

Overwhelmed by my tears, Tamara then said, "Tyrah get out the car. Let's go inside the house."

I get up and somehow I muster the strength to make it to the third floor of the apartment. I sit on the couch.

Tamara sits close to me and asks, "What happened?"

Part I

Chapter 1:

A Fearful Mindset

"She is clothed in strength and dignity and she laughs without fear of the future" -Proverbs 31:25

Bouncing Back to Me

*T*he future. I have always been the one who is afraid because of an uncertain future, wondering what God had planned for me. I have always wanted to know how I was going to get to the next-door waiting for me to open. Notice I said, "waiting for me to open". That was the problem. I thought I could do it all on my own. I thought being a go-getter and always wanting to stay one step ahead of everyone around me, was a good thing. It really didn't occur to me that I thought it was all about me. Yes, I was self-centered, judgmental, and at the same time, the perfect Christian daughter that every Christian parent would love to have. I walked like I knew I had it going on, but tried to keep it humble. I was a model for crying out loud! Who doesn't love to be around a model?

Bouncing Back to Me

By the age of 16, I had done so many pageants and held a couple of queen titles, but deep down, I was putting on a front. By the time I was a senior in high school, I was modeling almost every weekend for different local designers and runway events, but I didn't think I was pretty enough on the outside. On the outside it looked like I had it all together, but deep down I was dealing with some serious issues and insecurities. I couldn't afford the most expensive clothes that my fellow classmates had. I didn't have the nicest car like everyone had. I didn't have a boyfriend because the guy I wanted had other things going on. On top of all that, I was also afraid to leave high school to become an adult. Yet, day-by-day my time in high school was coming closer to the end.

My mind was always my worst enemy. The saying in church is, "If the devil can get your mind, he has you." It really is a true saying. Anything that could go wrong, I was

thinking it inside of my head. Everyone looked up to me,

but I had my own insecurities. I've always been a private

person, so I didn't really know who to talk to. I have a

loving family, but in my head, no one wanted to hear my

problems because I haven't lived long enough to know

exactly what a "problem" was. I knew who God was

because I was raised in the church my entire life. Doubting,

I asked myself, "God do you even care? I know I'm

blessed, but do you hear me"?

Chapter 2:

Growing Pains

"Train up a child in the way he should go; even when he is
old he will not depart from it." –Proverbs 22:6

Bouncing Back to Me

I grew up the youngest out of four children. My siblings, Brad, Fred and Tamara were already in high school by the time I was born. I always figured they had their own lives established and figured out so we didn't have anything in common because they were so much older. My brothers had moved to California, so I only had my sister in the house. Even with her being in the house, I often thought that having older siblings was equivalent to being an only child. My sister had her own friends, her own boyfriend, own life figured out. I was always with my parents.

My mom is a gospel-recording artist so growing up, we were always traveling somewhere so she could minister. I never got tired of it. My mom was a superhero to me. She was the best singer in the world in my eyes and I was her biggest fan. I loved seeing the audience react to her singing.

Bouncing Back to Me

I bragged to all my peers in elementary school. Who else's mom has such amazing vocals? My sister was her "mini me". Tamara also has vocals out of this world. The two of them often performed duets. Watching the two of them would make my day. It was also the first time when my mind first started going all over the place. Why couldn't it be a trio? No one asked me to sing yet and if they did, I acted uninterested because I knew I couldn't sing like them. This was the beginning of a seemingly never-ending saga of the enemy trying to attack my mind.

I can sing a little, but I am nowhere close to the powerhouses my mom and sister are. Not them alone, but my entire family on my mom's side are all musically inclined. My grandfather was the pioneer. His voice was so smooth that it reminded me of Al Green and Marvin Gaye mixed together. He taught my uncles how to play several instruments and my mom and aunt how to sing. He was in several gospel groups. I'd like to think that my mom's family was the gospel version of The Jackson 5. My grandmother couldn't sing, but like Catherine Jackson, she gave birth to some talented singers and musicians. From the stories I've been told, my grandfather didn't play about his rehearsals. I believe he really had the talent to become famous had he pursued it.

My sister received the gift of singing. Brad and Fred were both very good at rapping. So I was often secretly jealous that I didn't get to sing with my family. Singing just wasn't my talent and knowing that, I sometimes lacked confidence and had trouble finding my own way.

My parents tried putting me into different activities. I secretly hated all of them, but they both supported everything I tried. They still do. Both of my parents are my biggest supporters. I never lasted long in anything they tried to put me in. At age seven, I quit ballet after two classes. At age 10, I quit karate after moving forward to yellow belt. At age 11, I quit sewing classes after making a blanket for my nephew who was almost one. I just wanted to sing but I didn't sound good. I was trying so desperately to find something that would make my parents proud.

This all changed one day when I turned on the TV and watched a show called, "America's Next Top Model" or ANTM, hosted by supermodel Tyra Banks. I always knew I was named after her, but didn't really understand why she was so popular. I knew she was a model, but that didn't really impress me. All I wanted to do was sing. However, after watching several episodes of ANTM, I was hooked. Everything about the show was impressive to me. All the ladies were beautiful. I thought to myself, "I believe

Bouncing Back to Me

I can do this!" It was in that moment, I felt that I had discovered my gift.

I told my mom that modeling was what I wanted to do. I think by this time, my parents didn't want to waste anymore money on activities if I wasn't going to commit, but my mom didn't show it on her face.

"Well if this is something that you really want to do let's do our research", said my mom.

We Googled everything modeling related. The main thing we researched was on building a model portfolio and making a comp card. One of the first things we learned is that a comp card is a collection of images used for commercial print, auditions and self-promotion. It has your specific measurements (height, weight, age, etc.) and photos that are used to market you as an actor or model. It

Bouncing Back to Me

became my goal to complete my first comp card like a true professional.

My mom had worked with a local wedding photographer and was able to book my first photoshoot. I was probably around the age of 12 at this time. You couldn't tell me anything that day. The shoot was scheduled at this fancy hotel near the Jacksonville Airport. I remember being so happy that day. I had been watching reruns of ANTM and practiced my poses that entire week. I just knew the photos would turn out great. And they did. I was so impressed. (Looking back at those photos now--- makes me cringe. But hey, I was only12, so back then they were nothing short of amazing to me). I remember thinking to myself, "I've found it. This is what I'm supposed to be doing." I've been doing it ever since.

Bouncing Back to Me

I thought because I had found my niche and modeling was my thing, I would easily be cool and very popular in middle school. That was hardly the case. I was teased so much for being different. I was the "church girl" to everyone. I wore glasses and I was super skinny with a squeaky voice. (I still have the squeaky voice at 23). No boys wanted to date me. I had become friends with all the "pretty girls" in school, but I didn't think that I was pretty. Certainly I wasn't because I didn't have a boyfriend and if a boy did like me, it was probably because someone told him to have pity on me. In fact, my best friend at the time, who I will refer to as Meagan, tried to hook me with up her friend whose name I don't even remember. He was so cute and he was older (seventh grade), so that was a plus. To make a long story short, he didn't like me and instead, the two of them began dating shortly afterwards. He told my friend that I looked too innocent. After all, he was a "thug" (That's what I was told and I believed it; because I seemed to think it was impressive to be a thug at such a young age). Now, I was in the sixth grade then. Looking back, I laugh so hard, because who is actually dating at 11 or 12-years-old? Yet, even at such a young age, we are led to believe that we should be which leads to so many young minds making mistakes.

But wait, how did that happen? Meagan insisted that she had no intentions of dating the boy and that it just happened that way. I couldn't be mad at her. I couldn't blame the guy for wanting to be with her. She was light skinned and super funny. I was brown-skinned, super awkward and holy. I didn't even cuss. In fact, no one in my family did. Who wants the awkward kid--- the "goody two-shoes"? No one. Right?

Bouncing Back to Me

Even at a young age, I knew there was a calling over my life. However, when you're young and getting teased you try to fit in. Now I embrace the originality that God has blessed me with, but back then I simply tried too hard to be like my peers.

Meagan was that girl that every guy wanted. We met in the third grade. She was spontaneous and fun to be around. She was a tomboy so everyone knew she was tough. We were two peas in a pod. Whenever I got picked on, Meagan was right there to defend me.

I remember her telling me in fifth grade, "You have to toughen up or else everyone will walk all over you." I took offense to it.

"I am tough! God got me. I'm not concerned with these kids!" But I was. We were so young and everyone around me had boyfriends. Every boy liked Meagan. Boys would come up to me all the time and ask me if I could put in a good word for them. "Sure," I would always respond.

"No. Tell him I already have a boyfriend," said Meagan. I remind you, we were in elementary school. I always had to be the bearer of bad news. It was exhausting for a 10-year-old.

When we left elementary school, I was separated from all of my friends. Meagan went off to a middle school for the arts and I was still trying to find my voice at Highlands Middle School. I hated that school. I believe every preteen goes through a rebellious phase. Highlands was full of "tough" kids. I had to be tough too in order to survive middle school. Meagan taught me that.

The first time a teacher called my mom was in the seventh grade. I started hanging around girls I knew were "off the chain" and "fast". They didn't even look like middle schoolers. They looked like seniors about to graduate high school, yet we were all turning 13 soon. My mom wasn't a fan of them.

"I don't like those girls you're hanging out with," she said.

"They're really cool, just trust me," I responded.

I was wrong. As usual Sabrina Walker was always right when it came down to whom I was hanging around. Parents see what we often miss. At first, you think that they're just being uptight and that they just don't want you to have fun in life. I always had the older parents out of all my friends. My mom was 35 and my dad was 41 when they had me, so I often felt that they just weren't young enough to understand the times we were living in. But with age comes wisdom. My parents always instilled in me to have a mind of my own. To always be a leader and never a follower.

Bouncing Back to Me

They taught me that being different was perfectly fine. My parents weren't perfect, but they tried. At that age, I just didn't want to listen.

"Your teacher called me today. She said she had to tell you and your friends to stop talking and disrupting class several times," my mom began to discuss my conduct for the day as she picked me up after school.

She continued in a more focused and stern voice, "She also said that your behavior seems to have changed. That you shouldn't be hanging around those girls. She see's something in you Tyrah. She can tell you have been raised in a good home."

"She just hates me. She doesn't like black people," I said--- knowing that wasn't the case. I just needed to blame it on something. My mom knew I was full of it.

Bouncing Back to Me

That's the thing with my mom. I could never hide when something was wrong. She could just look into my eyes and know when I've had a rough day or when something was bothering me. Whenever something was wrong, I tried so hard to smile it away, but even then, she knew. I could fool everyone else, but I could never fool my mom.

"I birthed you. I know when something is not right," she would say.

That was the first time I did a self-check. One of many that I would do in my life. I told myself that the girls I was hanging with were okay, because I wasn't like them. I was still a leader. They did things that I didn't do. I was still a good girl. But at that age, I didn't understand that the company you keep says a lot about you. Deep down I knew those girls were no good for me, but I wanted to be cool. I wanted to fit in. I wanted to be tough. Oh yeah, a boyfriend

would've been nice too!

Chapter 3:

New Perspectives

"Do you not know that your body is a temple of the Holy Spirit, who is in you, whom you have received from God? You are not your own; you were bought at a price. Therefore, honor God with your body." – 1 Corinthians 6:19-20

Bouncing Back to Me

*L*ooking back at it, I never understood my obsession with having a boyfriend. I was always surrounded by couples, whether it was the kids at my school, the young couples at church or my relatives. Here I was, age 13, and I thought if you had a boyfriend then your life was going pretty darn good. If you didn't, then you were a loser.

It was a fresh new start. By this time, my parents were separated and I was able to attend Mandarin Middle School. It was a school in a predominately white neighborhood, different than what I was familiar with. Most kids my age can't handle their parents splitting up. But I wasn't one of them. I knew my parents were better off separated. A fresh new start was what we needed. It was

Bouncing Back to Me

a difficult adjustment at first, but my mother and I managed to get through it by the grace of God. I'm not going to sugarcoat anything. Those were hard times. I had never seen my mother go through so much before. Seeing my superhero cry was hard for me to see. It was also hard financially. The struggle was real. However, God never left us. He made a way.

It was exciting to start a new school where no one knew me. No one would pick on me. Plus, I modeled so that was a bonus. I had the opportunity to make new friends and make a name for myself.

And there he was, walking the halls just as handsome as could be. He played football and basketball; and he was the finest boy in school. I'll refer to him as Jason. Jason was my first real crush. His smile was everything and then some. For the longest, I was so scared to talk to him. Every time he came up to one of my friends to talk, I'd just stand there looking scared. All the girls wanted Jason, but I wasn't every girl. I was different. My parents had always taught me that I was different. I stepped to him boldly one day and told him that I liked him. I didn't know anything about him. All I knew was that he was going to be my future boyfriend and you never step in the way of a girl that's on a mission.

"I like you too," he said. This is what I thought. Here we go. I'm being tough. I'm being bold.

"I like you as a friend though. We can be good friends," Jason said.

My heart sank. That was the first time I was friend-zoned. However, we were friends, and eventually that was fine by me. He wasn't that smart--- that was a major turn off for me. I'd like to think that I had dodged a bullet.

Bouncing Back to Me

My new school was great for me. I made friends that I still talk to this very day. I didn't get picked on, everyone treated me with kindness and knew I was one of the smartest girls in school. My best guy friend, Aaron, was a hot mess. He was everything you wouldn't want in a boyfriend. He was messy, annoying, stubborn, crazy and we argued pretty much every day. But that was my best friend, he had my back and I had his. If you weren't in our circle of friends, nothing bad had better come out your mouth about him and vice versa.

One day I asked him on the phone, "Why don't guys like me? Every time I try to be myself it just doesn't work."

Aaron said, "It's because you're not easy. Most guys only go after someone they know they can sleep with easily. You're not that kind of girl and guys aren't ready to settle down just yet. It's not serious for us at this age. And you're a virgin. It's not that they don't like you; they just know you're a good girl. That's something to be proud of."

That sat with me for a couple days. My mom had always told me what Aaron said, but coming from a guy, it put a lot of things into perspective. I took pride in being a virgin, but it wasn't something I told the whole world. I knew nothing about sex at 14. The thought made me cringe. A lot of the slang I knew, I learned at school by walking past "experienced students".

Being a virgin until marriage was something I was taught. Saving myself for the man God has for me was something I looked forward to. My sister was a virgin when she married, and I looked up to her. I had no desire. I didn't even know kids my age and younger were doing THAT. I never knew what temptation was like. I never put myself in those situations. After that conversation with Aaron, I felt better about myself. I somehow built up a little confidence that day. It meant a lot to me, because this was coming from someone that liked a different girl every day of the week. A lot of people asked me why am I still friends with him after all these years of his pettiness. Well because, no one knows how much his response to my question helped me in a major way. I would still battle with my singleness as I grew older and entered my high school years, but his answer was constantly in the back of my head.

I always knew I had a calling on my life. My mom told me about a dream she had when she was pregnant with me. The dream was about witches trying to take me away from her. She said she pled the blood of Jesus and woke up. I knew I was not like the other kids and I think that hurt more knowing that. I didn't know then that sometimes in this journey you have to walk alone. Now that I'm older I understand that you're never truly alone. God will never leave you nor forsake you. He is always there in a time of need. But during that phase in my life, I struggled to believe that He was there. Comparisons are what I struggled with the most during my senior year of highschool, but we'll get to that later.

Chapter 4:

Crowns

"Her value is more precious than jewels and her worth is
far above rubies or pearls." Proverbs 31:10

Bouncing Back to Me

igh school. The first day it begins, high school is a journey all by itself. I went to Wolfson High School, and I hated it my freshman year. It was another fresh new start, but I missed all my friends at Mandarin Middle. They all went to Mandarin High School and that wasn't my school zone. I was nervous to be in high school, but I had honors classes, so I already knew my future was bright.

By my sophomore year, I had made a name for myself. I was the smart kid. My older cousin was on the football team and everyone knew not to mess with me. I can almost guarantee I was annoying to him, but I enjoyed having someone that secretly had my back even though he wouldn't show it around his friends. My friends, Alexys and Kia, were my right hands. We were not alike in any way, but we balanced each other out. They kept me in check when I was wrong and vice versa.

Tenth grade was also the year when I began doing pageants. I was still modeling here and there, but when people ask me how I started modeling professionally, pageants are always my response. My first pageant was Miss Jacksonville Teen USA and I lost. I was so excited leading up to this pageant and I felt like a hopeless case. I felt as if my dreams were being shattered right in front of me. First off, the pageant was expensive and living with a divorced mom, I knew she didn't have the money. However, my parents have worked hard in order for me to live my dreams. When I lost that pageant, much of my confidence went down. I had worked so hard. I knew nothing about pageants, but I knew I was different. I knew I was beautiful and I knew that I had what it took to win. I got caught up in the hype. I had gotten the "big head" before I did the pageant. I cried all night. How did I let this happened? How could I let my family down? They spent money that they didn't have, and I lost. I learned a valuable lesson that day. God will allow you to be brought down a few notches in order to teach you something. I was truly humbled on that day.

That was the first time I realized that God puts us through some situations in order to make us stronger. I thought I had all the confidence in the world in that pageant, but secretly, I was intimidated by the fact that I was the only black girl in the pageant. We're living in a time now where black women are learning how to celebrate themselves, even when no one else wants to celebrate us. This is "Black Girl Magic" season. Black women have always had it hard. We are at a double disadvantage to white women and the entire male population. We are stereotyped as "the Mammy" and "the Jezebel". We are told that we are mean and angry for no reason at all. We are told that we are too sexual, too "extra", too loud and too uptight. We have been degraded since slavery in the public eye.

What does it mean to be magical? Magic is when a black woman can wear her curly hair on Monday, straighten it on Tuesday, wear a wig on Thursday, and have it back curly by Saturday. Magic is when a black woman can stand strong inside a corporate meeting in a room full of white people and still hold her own and not be intimidated. Magic is when a group of black women can go out to lunch, talk for hours about their dreams and ambitions without anyone being jealous of the next black woman. Magic is when a black woman can voice her opinion without fear of being stereotyped as angry. Magic is when a black woman is the first one of her family to graduate from college with a 4.0 and a Doctorate degree. Magic is when a black woman finally decides she's not going to settle for less than what she deserves from a man. Magic is when a black woman makes it, because sometimes that all she knows how to do. Magic is when a black woman can admit her weaknesses and brings her troubles to God without shame.

Well, I didn't know about that magic just yet when I lost the pageant. The money I spent on weave for that pageant. The money I did not have. The stress I endured when I saw all the other girls had blonde hair and blue eyes. How was I supposed to win, when the odds were already set against me? And certainly, they were not going to give it to another black girl because one had just won the year before.

When you fall down, it's up to you whether you stay on the ground or get up and continue moving toward your destiny. I had been so used to succeeding in many areas of my life. This experience humbled me like never before. See, when you get to a place where you think no one can tell you anything. God will humble you really quickly, and boy was I humbled on that day.

I could've let that first pageant stop me from ever competing again, but I didn't stop there. I decided to compete again, this time in Daytona Beach, Florida; another pageant lost. However, this time, I was getting pageant help and I even had a pageant coach. My confidence level was way higher than it was the first time. It wasn't until my third pageant in Melbourne, Florida that

Bouncing Back to Me

I won my first title: Miss Melbourne Teen USA and I was the first African-American to do so.

A lot of good came out of doing pageants. I loved working with young girls and giving advice. After winning Miss Melbourne Teen USA, I went to the next round to compete in Miss Florida Teen USA. I was so ready for this. I was determined to win. My pageant coach and I were so excited. We just knew that I would at least make the top 10.

The big pageant was held in Miami, FL, 56 girls in total and only one other black girl besides myself. All the judges were white middle-aged women. Long story short, I did not win. I didn't even make the top 14. Devastated yet again. I remember feeling how I felt during my first pageant, only worse. The day before the pageant was the preliminaries and I felt unstoppable. Not in a conceited type of way, I just felt good about myself. I felt good about my interview and I came with a different look. I cried but not in front of the others ladies. Wise advice I had received from my family a few days before: If you have to cry, you better go to a restroom or somewhere far away from everyone else. You never let them see you cry. I made sure I didn't let them see me cry. When I went inside the restroom, I cried. I cried so much my face went numb.

"You should've been in that top 14. This whole thing is rigged," my mom said after the pageant.

The year prior, a black girl had won Miss Florida Teen USA. It was unheard of back then to allow back-to-back black girls to win a pageant. But to not let, at least one of the only two black girls in the pageant, into the top 14 was still just so weird to me. We were good contestants, yet at least one of us deserved to be on that stage. Thankfully, times have changed since 2011. Imagine my surprise when I recently watched Miss USA to see five black women in the top 10, back-to-back black titleholders, and both with natural hair. I cried. That moment was for the culture.

My problem was I thought that would be the end of my "shine". Little did I know, God was preparing me for something much greater than I could see. My modeling jobs increased tremendously. I gained more connections and opportunities in the business than ever before. I was proud of myself for all the hard work I was accomplishing. In life, there will be lessons that you have to go through in order to tell someone else your story. My story was just beginning. The next phase of my life would be my biggest trial to experience. I didn't know that I would soon battle depression in the form of a toxic relationship.

Chapter 5:

The
Beginning

"Like a city whose walls are broken through is a person who lacks self-control" Proverbs: 25:28

Bouncing Back to Me

We met through mutual friends when we were 13. Bryan liked me from the moment our eyes met, but I didn't like him originally. I just wanted to be friends. He was very nice from the beginning, but I could tell he was probably the player type. We would see each other here and there as the years went by, when we were both with our mutual friends. I remember him texting me one day expressing his love for me and how much he really liked me. We were freshmen, but went to different high schools.

"Okay. I just like you as a friend," I responded back. It was cruel looking back at it. My sister always told me I had a thing for dissing the guys that really liked me, and liking the ones that didn't pay any attention. She was right, but I never wanted to admit when people were right, until after the damage had been done.

Bouncing Back to Me

He would continue to like me, but I wouldn't budge until later.

I went on liking the not so good guys until I finally said to myself, "I'm just going to be single. It's time to enjoy my life. I'm doing so well right now."

By junior year of high school, I was pretty content with my single life. I was just an independent woman at this point. One day I was on Facebook and heard Bryan's music for the first time. I was so impressed with his rapping skills. He had never told me that he was an artist. I immediately hit him up to tell him how great his song was and how proud I was of him. He was always telling me how proud he was of my endeavors and my modeling. We often gave each other compliments, so I didn't think this one would be any different.

Bouncing Back to Me

Then it hit me. I had spent so much time worrying about guys that didn't like me, not realizing Bryan was into me since the moment we met. I never gave him a chance and I felt really bad about it. I didn't tell him right away though. I waited for a while, because I didn't want it to seem as if I only liked him once I found out he could rap and sing. It may seem that way, but it truly wasn't. It was as if a light bulb had switched on in my head. We texted each other every day after that. I started to like him each day just a little bit more.

"Why all of a sudden the interest?" Bryan finally asked. I knew it wouldn't be long before he asked.

"I just regret not giving you a chance when I first met you," I responded. "Granted, we were children so I don't know if it would've lasted three years by now; so maybe there was a reason why I didn't like you at first."

Bouncing Back to Me

He was cool and he was smooth. His smile was perfect. We had a lot in common, and we'd talk for hours at a time on the phone.

What I didn't know was that he had a girlfriend. Wow! That was just my luck. I should've snatched him when I had the chance. Well, it was too late now. I wasn't the type of girl that dated guys with girlfriends. I had a pure heart. I wasn't going that route and I knew he wasn't like that either. The attraction was still there and we both tried to escape it. I felt like I had missed out on a great relationship. He was my friend first, so we could both hold ourselves together.

But that first kiss. It happened unintentionally. It was just casual conversation. It came out of nowhere. I didn't even realize it until minutes later that I had kissed a guy that already had a girlfriend. My head was spinning. I had felt so horribly wrong. He did too. What was going on? How did a casual conversation lead to a peck on the lips?

We tried to ignore each other. We tried to ignore our feelings for each other. We tried. Lord knows, I honestly tried. But somehow we became closer to the point I called him my best friend. At times, it felt that he was my only supporter. He listened for hours about my dreams and ambitions. He encouraged me to not be afraid to try out new things. He was the third person I contacted after winning Senior Class President, after my mom and dad. We were that close. I told him everything about me and vice versa. He knew everything, including my fears. He was simply my best friend.

My entire family knew him and I loved his family. They were cool people. We hung out all the time. My family would ask me why we weren't dating. I couldn't tell them that I was starting to fall for someone who was already taken. Already taken. I knew he liked me just as much, but he was still taken. A part of me wanted to stop talking to him completely. He was my best friend. He cared for me and I cared about him.

"If a guy really wants to be with you, he will do everything in his power to make sure it will happen," my mom had told me multiple times when I came to her about any new boy I liked.

That always stayed with me. It was like every time I found myself liking Bryan, her words would resonate within me and would not go away. To this day, I live by those words. And yet, I wrestled with those words during this time period. He wasn't in a position to be with me, because he was a good guy. You know how women do from time-to-time. We go against our gut. We make excuses for the men we're involved with. We ignore God. I ignored God. I knew my worth as a Christian woman, but somehow I still ignored God. My feelings for him were too deep.

It was prom season. Of course I couldn't go with him because he was with another girl. Imagine me having to explain that to my family.

"I have to make something up," I thought to myself. "No I can't because I don't lie to my family. They know everything. (Honestly, I think they knew the real reason why Bryan couldn't take me to the prom, but they didn't want to tell me that they knew).

I wasn't going to prom empty handed, I knew that. My god-sister had introduced me to a friend of hers. He was tall, athletic, smart and very attractive. He took me on a date and seemed like the perfect guy. He treated me exceptionally well. Michael was everything you probably would want in a significant other. I couldn't see that though. I was too busy worrying about Bryan. During this difficult time in my life, I tried to date other people. I tried to step out of my comfort zone, but I always found something negative with whomever I was involved with. Michael was no different.

He took me to my prom and we also went to his prom the week after. He was conservative and came from a great family. His brother was my little pal. "This could work," I remember thinking to myself. Bryan himself told me that Michael would be good for me. They went to the same school. They knew each other well. Deep down within, I knew that Bryan didn't want to see me with anyone else, but he finally knew how it felt. Knowing this, secretly made me feel better.

Bouncing Back to Me

"So you and Bryan kissed before?" Michael asked me. Oh shoot! I thought. Who told him this? No one except for Alexys knew this. (Alexys knew my every move back then. She was non-judgmental and that's what I love about her the most. She was disappointed in me for sure, but she never judged me.)

"How do you know that?" Here I was ready to curse Bryan out for telling my business. I just knew he was trying to sabotage my prom date since he couldn't take me, but it wasn't him. Michael and Bryan's then girlfriend were close. Bryan was honest about us. I respected him for that although it made me feel worse. Now to this day, I'm not sure how the conversation between Bryan's ex and Michael went, but somehow Michael found out and I expected him to be mad about it, but he wasn't. He was just waiting for me to say something. He didn't want to hear any he-say or she-say, so I told him the truth. I assured him that Bryan and I were only friends and he had nothing to worry about. I knew it was going to happen, but imagine my surprise when I found out we would all be at the same dinner table including a bunch of people I didn't know. Just perfect! Why did we have to go to both proms? Couldn't mine just suffice? I guess that would be selfish. I used to be the queen of selfish.

What a horrible situation to be in. I had nothing to worry about at my prom. Except the agony I knew I was about to face leading up to Michael's prom, knowing that Bryan would be there with his date.

Bryan and I talked the day before the prom. We promised that this experience would not affect our friendship. If we could get through the prom, we could get through anything for sure. Besides, I wanted to really try things out with Michael. I wanted the feelings for Bryan to go away.

I ruined my chances with Michael. I know I did. My prom went perfectly, but his didn't end well. I had gone through the night not really paying Bryan and his date any mind. Once Michael took me home, I couldn't help but wonder what they were doing.

"I had a great time Bryan," I said as Michael was taking me home.

Oh my God. How did I just call this young man by the wrong name? I immediately thought, I must be the stupidest person to ever walk the earth. I had to quickly think of a good reason as to why I accidentally called him another guy's name. Long story short, I never heard from Michael again. He had every right not to talk to me.

Bouncing Back to Me

There are still times that I think about prom night. If my mind was not so consumed with Bryan, things could've worked out with Michael. There would be many times during this period in my life that I wished it did, but it was far too late.

Chapter 6:

Back and Forth

"For God is not a God of confusion but of peace."
1 Corinthians 14:33

Bouncing Back to Me

Bryan was single one moment. He was taken again the next moment. He was single for the second time around. He was taken again weeks later. I couldn't keep up. Back and forth. Back and forth. One moment he would be with me, the next with her. Even when he was "with me", he didn't make it official. I would think to myself, "what is wrong with me? What does she have that I don't?" How did I let it get to this point? How could I have been so stubborn? I don't believe in zodiac signs, but I couldn't help myself during this time period. Taurus' are known for being stubborn people. We hate change. I've been asked why I stayed around for so long and that would be my answer every time. "I hate change." There was another reason as to why I stayed too.

Bouncing Back to Me

He was the only guy that respected my virginity. I remember having that conversation with him. I simply told him that I was not giving it up until I got married. He was perfectly fine with it. I was the one of the few virgins he knew that was committed to waiting till marriage. That had never happened before. You know, you meet certain guys and then the moment you let your virginity be known, they basically run the other direction. But not Bryan. He was willing to compose himself, because our love was much deeper than sex. We had far too many others things we enjoyed doing that kept our minds off of it, like attending open mic nights and going to the movies almost every weekend. Sure there would be temptation every now and then, but he respected me and knew how important it was for me to reach my goal. To this day, I thank him for that because he could've easily led me on or taken advantage of me, but he didn't.

We argued all the time. Many of our arguments had a lot to do with my trust issues about him. Certainly I couldn't trust him, because he liked me when he was with his ex, so now that he was single (the moments he was), I was always wondering whom he was with, where he was going and how long he was doing what he was doing. Additionally, social media was a problem. Now, I'm a private person when it comes to my relationships, and I try to keep my social media strictly about my career, but I'm one of those people that doesn't see the harm in posting your significant other a few times. It seemed like he never wanted me to post him and I had to beg just to get featured on at least a Snap Chat post. Was he ashamed of me? Was he worried about what his ex and her friends would say?

Bouncing Back to Me

He posted her all the time when they were together and had no shame in doing so. He didn't care if I saw it or not. He did what he wanted to do. So why was it a problem with me? This is when my depression hit. This is when I started comparing myself to other people.

Chapter 7:

Comparisons

"For I am confident of this very thing, that He who began a good work in you will perfect it until the day of Christ Jesus." Philippians 1:6

Bouncing Back to Me

hen you compare yourself to other people, you start forgetting the person God made you to be. You forget about the blessings God has given to you. You forget about everything and start wasting your time on things that don't concern you. You start thinking of yourself as less than or inferior to the next person. Somehow everything you've ever accomplished goes out the window, instantly. You waste hours and hours of precious time, comparing yourself to someone who's not even thinking twice about you.

That's how it was. I started comparing myself to Bryan's ex. I started paying attention to the way he was with her, versus with me. It consumed my days. I constantly checked her Instagram and Twitter accounts, at least three times a day. It sounds like I was stalking, but I was comparing myself. I started feeling that I wasn't pretty compared to her. I started thinking that Bryan must've kept going back to her, because her natural hair was bigger than mine. She must've been funnier than me too. I started asking questions to people that I knew personally who also knew her. I wanted to know as much as possible so I could figure out why he wouldn't treat me the way I needed to be treated.

In doing that, I lost my identity. People told me all the time how proud they were of me and how much success I had with modeling. But, I had other things on my mind. Sure I knew that had a bright future ahead of me and I was doing more fashion shows and photoshoots than I could keep up with, but my mind was elsewhere. Bryan was on my mind all the time. It consumed me. I was slowly losing my focus on who I was. I started not to recognize myself in the mirror. I cried. I cried all the time. My face would be

Bouncing Back to Me

constantly swollen or puffy because of the tears. My weight

was also a problem. I had lost so much weight; I looked

frail, almost malnutritious. My collarbone looked like it

was going to pop out of my body. My parents made me

drink Ensure to help me gain weight, but it didn't work. I

put on a front. I had on a mask that I didn't want to take

off. I didn't understand how I got to this point. I admired

my sister and her husband. I just wanted their type of

relationship. I secretly envied every couple that came

across my screen. I wanted Bryan to be my mine and mine

only.

I never wanted to think of myself as the "side chick". I

had too much class for that. But being real, that's how I felt

and probably how it was, but he never allowed me to call

myself that. Bryan genuinely had a good heart and was a

wonderful person, but we both had a lot a growing up to do.

Bouncing Back to Me

My mom always told me that you constantly have to pray over your mind, because that's the one place the devil can easily influence you. Once he has taken over your mind, he has you. I was depressed all the time. I would try to hide it from the person that knew me the best, my mom. I could get nothing past her. Often times she would know how sad I was, but never forced me to talk about anything. She would just let me cry on her shoulder until I was ready to talk about what was on my mind. One day I saw a picture of Bryan and his ex on Instagram after he told me they were just friends. Her caption appeared to be more than just friends. That night, I cried myself to sleep on my mom's shoulders. I showed her the picture and the tears poured out.

Bouncing Back to Me

I shouted, "Mom how can he lie to me like this?" The tears flowed like a river. My nose was stuffy, my eyes were red and my body ached.

As I reflect on what happened, I can only imagine how horrible my mom must have felt to see her baby girl go through so much pain. She kept wiping the tears from my eyes with her hands. The tears kept pouring down my face faster than she could wipe away. It was almost like I was a newborn baby fresh out the womb. Crying more than I could breathe. Then my mom did what she always does. She sung to me. She started singing, "Break Every Chain" by Tasha Cobbs. Her voice is one of the smoothest voices I've ever heard. That night was no different. I'm pretty sure I feel asleep to the calmness of her voice.

I knew I was bigger and better than this. That still, small voice in my head kept telling me to get up out of my dark place. However, no matter how many times I heard that voice, I stayed in my dark place. It's so easy to stay in that place once you're there. You have no energy left. You can't truly tell people everything you're going through because you know they wouldn't understand. You don't want people judging you or talking about you, so you let the emotions get the best of you. You just know that God is upset with you, so you don't even bother talking to him about it because in your mind, he doesn't want to hear it. You start believing everything is your fault. You ignored the signs that were there in the beginning, and since you ignored those signs, now you feel as if you're stuck and can't get out. In the beginning of 2018, I read a book written by Tyler Perry, "Higher is Waiting". In one of the chapters, Perry wrote about the deep roots that caused him to make the same mistakes in life although he wanted to change. What were the generational curses or generational events that occurred within his family? I started thinking about the deep roots in my life. Why have relationships always been trouble for me? Why did I stay so long with Bryan when I was younger? Then it hit me. I saw it growing up.

My late grandmother went through so much with my late grandfather. She went through verbal abuse for as long as I could remember growing up. Why did she stay and put up with that mistreatment? Was it fear? I never understood. My mother. She stayed in a marriage so long even when she wanted out. My dad is the best father in the world, but they just couldn't get along. My mom stayed so long out of fear of what others would say, fear that she wouldn't be able to make it on her own. Fear.

Bouncing Back to Me

As I read that chapter it all made sense. It was fear of being alone. I wish I had known then what I know now.

"Well I don't want to start over," I'd think to myself. "If I meet someone new, I'd have to tell them all about myself and ask stupid questions to get to know them too." I had gotten comfortable.

Afraid of change. Afraid to get uncomfortable. One of the songs that helped me was "Uncomfortable" by my favorite rapper Andy Mineo. His whole album talked about being comfortable and how dangerous that can be. In this daily walk in Christ, we have to get uncomfortable. Webster's Dictionary defines *uncomfortable* as, "causing uneasiness". How are we to grow if we get comfortable in the same mindset that we're in? If there is no growth, you will constantly see the same results every time. No matter how hard I tried to make my relationship work with Bryan,

Bouncing Back to Me

I kept experiencing the same results. The same hurt over and over again. The same tears flowed from my face every night.

I learned that when we're too comfortable in the same position, we become unfocused. We tend to get lazy and stay in the same position for years, sometimes decades. It drains us, but we stay right there. We know we should be experiencing more, but we're scared to take that leap of faith. I was scared to take that leap. The phases when Bryan and I weren't together, I was scared to be alone. I was scared of being single. I thought I just had to have someone take my mind away from him. So I would try to talk to different guys, but my mind wasn't in the right place because I was doing it all for the wrong reasons. I wanted him to be jealous. I wanted him to know how it felt to be in love with someone who is in love with someone else.

Bouncing Back to Me

It then occurred to me that this was the time for me to be on my face, in my prayer closet and crying out to the Lord. At first, I missed those opportunities. I was going to everyone, except God. I was ignoring Him when I could've gone to Him from the beginning. You know how people say, "When you're really tired of going through, you will stop what you're doing?" I hadn't reached that moment just yet because I was still going back every time. I was still allowing myself to be upset. I was not recognizing that I am the daughter of a King. Instead, I allowed myself to stay in a dark place that was very difficult to get out.

PART II

Chapter 8:

Sister, Sister

"A friend loves at all times, and a brother [sister] is born for a time of adversity" Proverbs: 17:17

Bouncing Back to Me

I told Tamara everything that happened. Well looking back at it, I didn't tell her everything that I went through because I felt she would've looked at me differently. She would've judged me. She would've been disappointed in her little sister that I stayed around as long as I did. At that time, I thought I was telling her everything. Tamara and I are so far apart in age that if it weren't for that, I would've opened up to her a long time ago. Growing up with the rest of your siblings being out of the house and living their adult life discouraged me a lot. Oh how I wish I had grown up with them. Being the youngest, I didn't tell my siblings anything at all really. My sister knew more about my life than my brothers, but that's just because I saw her on a regular basis. Still, I grew up not having siblings close to my age to listen to me vent. I talked to myself as a child. That's how I gave myself advice sometimes. I talked to myself and would come up with possible conclusions.

But now, I was talking to my sister. This was my moment to get everything off of my chest. I knew I could count on my sister, because she had gone through similar situations with her ex-boyfriend. I was too young to remember everything, but I thought to myself that she would know what to do.

Transparency. That's what I love the most. People that are not afraid to tell others about the things they have gone through and how it made them stronger. My sister took the time to be transparent with me. She told me all about what she went through as an early college student and her previous relationship. I needed to hear everything she had

Bouncing Back to Me

to say. She reminded me of my worth. I had forgotten who I was. I had forgotten how much of a Queen I truly was.

Tamara knew how much I loved Bryan. It was written all over my face. Somehow, I had gotten to the point to where I was broken and trying to put myself together. It was as if I was a broken vase. I had never cried so much before that day, before that moment.

"Tyrah, he's not going to leave her," Tamara said with all the heart a big sister could give to an inexperienced younger sister. "They'll probably get married. You never know. But you have to know your worth. You have to get up and know that God has someone that he created just for you. The person you're supposed to be with will not hurt you on purpose. The person you're supposed to be with will love you and only you. You don't deserve this and you don't need to be dealing with this. You are young and have plenty of time to be in a relationship. You are intelligent. You have so many things going for you. Look at you! You are a model and there's so much more in store for you than for you to be worrying about this."

Of course, I knew all of that. I knew before she told me. However, the words coming out of her mouth did something to me. It made me listen. We had never had a moment like this together. A part of me was shocked because this was the first time I had gone to her about my life's issues. She was my hero that day.

Tamara told me, "Get all the crying out now, because tomorrow is a brand new day. Tomorrow you're going to get up, get dressed and walk out the door with confidence. You are beautiful Tyrah."

I left her house feeling a little better. I was so happy that I had finally let out all the emotions and shared how I was

Bouncing Back to Me

feeling. I have always been a private person, but it felt so good letting it all out. I felt revived. I felt like I could move on from this. I felt like I could go on without it bothering me. I had come to the conclusion that it was time for me to wipe away the tears and start getting back on the right track. I had started looking a little rough around the edges during that time. I didn't take the time to do my hair, I didn't care what I had on (not sure if I even matched), I didn't bother to put on makeup, and overall I just didn't feel the need to look my best. However, the next morning when it was time to go to class, I decided to fix myself up. I put on a cute outfit, threw my wig on, put some makeup on my once puffy face, (even though at that time I was no where near as decent as I am now).

Bouncing Back to Me

I remember telling myself that this is it. This is the day that I get back to me. This is the day where I never speak to Bryan again. This is the day.

A few days later, Bryan sent me a text apologizing. I had forgiven him. It was a long text. By this time, he had moved to Atlanta, so I didn't see him as much. I figured we could still be friends. I could still forgive him and not want to be with him right? It's not like I could see him on a regular basis. Out of sight, out of mind right? Wrong. Despite that much needed talk with my sister, I had slowly let him back in. We didn't talk much at first after the apology, but it eventually crept in. A small conversation via text eventually led to longer conversations on the phone and a longing for our talks. Yes, I ended up missing him again. I started thinking to myself, "what had changed?" He seemed as if he had. I was still mad at what he put me

Bouncing Back to Me

through. I was still mad at the fact that it seemed as if he cared more for his ex than he did for me. I was still mad that we constantly went back and forth. I was still mad. But, it seemed as if he had changed. It seemed as if his focus was completely on me now. Should I take the risk and see for myself or let him go for good?

Chapter 9:

New City, Same Mind

"Brother's, I do not consider that I have made it my own. But one thing I do: forgetting what lies behind and reaching forward to what lies ahead, I press on toward the goal for the prize of the upward call of God in Christ Jesus." Philippians 3: 13-14

Bouncing Back to Me

I chose the first option. Everything in my gut was telling me that he and I would never work out, but I saw some changes in the way he treated me which made me go back. We were getting along better than ever. It was as if we were 13 again and had met for the first time. It was as if we were starting off fresh. No other people, just us.

I moved to Tampa. I transferred from the local state college to the University of South Florida after I received my Associates Degree. I left after Christmas break of 2016. The entire break was lovely spending time with Bryan. We were really on great terms and I began to feel as if we could move pass all of our troubles in the past.

My mom knew. She didn't agree with it, but she put up with it, just as my dad had. My dad would tell me that he knew how some guys were because he was like that at an early age. My dad never sugarcoated anything.

I didn't want my sister to know because she had spent so much time helping me that I didn't want to disappoint her. I didn't want her to think that our conversation was in vain.

Moving to Tampa to further my education was one of the best decisions I've ever made. It was a hard adjustment at first, but eventually, I found my way and fell in love with the campus. I had joined an organization that made me feel welcome. I had also joined the gospel choir that allowed me to keep my focus on a spiritual level. I was thrilled. There was just one thing. Bryan had started getting distant when I moved. We told each other that we wouldn't get distant. We would make time to talk to each other, if not every day, at least every other day. I am a strong believer that you make time for the people you care about no matter how busy you may be. I made time for him. I made sure that I at least sent an "I love you" text every night before I went to sleep. He instead, became distant from me. I heard from him less and less. I would barely even get a text back. The emotions started up again. The tears came back.

"Here we go again", I thought to myself. "Here we freaking go again!"

It was bad enough that I didn't get to see him all the time with him being in Atlanta and I in Tampa. The phone was literally all we had and he was ruining it. How did I let this happen again? I was miserable. I hated feeling this way. Here I was trying to find my way at a brand new school, but I couldn't help but think about what Bryan was doing and who he was spending his time with. Did I trust him? At times, I really did. In fact, there were times I totally forgot about the hurt he caused me. Except when he wouldn't call or text back for days, my mind would wander. It would think the worst.

When I thought the worst, we argued. One would think we were married the way we argued. Sometimes I told him off. Now if you know me really well, you know I am as sweet as can be. Just don't test me. I will tell you off and repent afterwards. The both of us would argue hard. I never listened to what he had to say. I just had to get in the last word. That was a major problem with us. I always wanted the last word. In the beginning we had great communication, but around this time, our conversation was dead and could not be resurrected.

I didn't know what I was capable of achieving until the following Fall semester attending USF. I was meeting people from all areas of life. I was hanging out with people that I never would've thought about hanging out with. I was embracing my natural self. I had found a church to attend and was spiritually growing into the godly woman I've always dreamed of being. I was tired of the arguments and hadn't heard from Bryan in a long time. I was ready for change. I was ready for God to restore me. My pastor at my Tampa church spoke a message about moving, advancing to your next level.

He said, "In order to advance, you first have to *admit*. You can't advance if you don't know where you currently are. You also have to *adjust* like a camera trying to get focused on an object. Adjust for distinct vision. Lastly, you have to *abandon* and leave everything behind that does not align with the will of God."

Wow. It hit me like a baseball hits a windshield of a car in a parking lot during a baseball game. I never told Pastor

Bouncing Back to Me

Francis Maxwell, but God was using him that day to speak to me. It was as if I was the only member in the church and he was speaking directly to me. The entire sermon just hit home with me. I took so many pages of notes that day. Everything that I had gone through in life all came rushing back to me in that moment. The tears flowed down my face faster than I could wipe them away.

"Yes Jesus, I hear you," I said to myself. "I hear you and I repent for all my sins. I repent for not listening to you. I repent for allowing this to go on as long as it has. I repent for not trusting you. I repent for not knowing how strong I truly was. I repent for ignoring all the signs that you gave me. I repent for being disobedient. I'm sorry Lord. I love you. Thank you for never giving up on me. Thank you for keeping me even when I wanted to lose my mind."

Bouncing Back to Me

I cried out so loud in church that day. I felt like all the old had lifted up off of me. I had rededicated my life to Christ on that day as well. It was time for me to finally advance. I ended things with Bryan for good.

It would take some time for me to really get over Bryan, but I was becoming a work in progress. I am a firm believer that time heals all wounds. I started smiling more. I started loving myself more. When I got dressed and made up everyday it's because I wanted to. I wanted to look good for myself, not for some young man. I started hanging out with my friends more. It felt good not to argue. It felt good going to sleep at night without worrying about what someone was doing. I had something more. I had joy.

Sure there were times that I felt lonely. In those times, I read my Bible. I went to movies alone; order a large popcorn and soda. I would take myself shopping or go home to visit my family. I tried not to dwell in that lonely place.

Bryan and I occasionally checked on each other, but for the most part, it was understood that the two of us had grown apart. We had brand new things going on and that was okay. At first, it was a tough pill to swallow, but it got easier with time. I will say that Bryan was never a horrible person. He has a heart of love and compassion for people. We just were not meant to be. We started off the wrong way. Even when I knew he was taken, the day he told me we still messed up and kissed each other. Our feelings got in the way. In fact, we were both at fault. That's why it didn't work out, when it was finally just the two of us. You reap what you sow. I had reaped, but I repented. I had taken a hard fall, but I had gotten up. God is not going to bless mess. You can pray all day long, but he simply will not

Bouncing Back to Me

bless things that are out of his will. Don't make the same

mistakes that I once did. Bryan is a wonderful person, and I

wish him nothing but the best in life. When you can truly

forgive a person, it frees you. You don't feel bound and

that person does not have any control over you any longer.

Chapter 10:

Black Girl Magic

"Better is open rebuke than hidden love. Wounds from a friend can be trusted, but an enemy multiplies kisses." Proverbs 27:5-6

Bouncing Back to Me

*J*ust when you feel as if you are alone in this love thing, God will show you that you are not. My crew, we call ourselves "Black Girl Magic" aka (BGM). I believe they were sent into my life at the perfect time. Taylor, Brielle, Ty'ra, Allana and Lindsey, are all women of God. We come from diverse beginnings in life (or backgrounds). We all have different personalities and interests. However, we all model or do something fashion-industry related. With that, we each have our different goals in life but still support one another.

It all started at my twenty-first birthday dinner. I had known each of them separately, but had invited all of them to my dinner. I've known Allana since I was a child, I met Brielle in Miami at a fashion show, I met Ty'ra at my previous state college (even though she looked as if she didn't like me at first), and then I met Taylor and Lindsey (sisters) through Allana. You would've thought that we had all been best friends for years. My birthday night started something legendary. Before you knew it, these ladies were like additional sisters. We listen to each other's problems, give each other words of wisdom, support each other at our individual events, and joke with one another. They also played a huge role helping me move on from my relationship with Bryan. The more time I spent with them, the more I began to realize that I'm still young and I have plenty of time to worry about relationships.

I believe society has taught us that in order to be successful in life, you must first hurry to get married, and have lots of babies. At first, that was my mission in life. I couldn't wait to get married and start a family. In high school, I honestly thought I would be married by now. But

Bouncing Back to Me

I have learned, I am in my prime and I have plenty of time to get married.

Society and the media can do a lot of damage to a person who is not spiritually or mentally in the right place. On Instagram we see images of beautiful women who have had surgeries and become Instagram models, and we think that their lives are better than ours. Celebrities are committing suicide and we think because they have "money" that they are not allowed to be depressed. Depression does not choose the poorest person. Depression is real and can attack anyone. You have to have on the full armor of God and recognize the devil's schemes. The enemy three jobs: to kill, steal and destroy.

I want to be able to focus on my career without any distractions. I want to go on road trips with friends and travel to different countries. I want to write more books. I

Bouncing Back to Me

want to get everything that God has for me. I want to live
my best life. I want to go to sleep peacefully at night
knowing I don't have to answer to anyone. I choose to be
happy. I'm okay right now with it just being me or casually
going out on dates; because when you're single, that's what
you do. The best relationships, in my opinion, are the ones
that you don't see coming. That's how I want it to be. I
used to wake up in the mornings wondering if I would meet
the man of my dreams. I was always the single one out of
my friends, so I felt as if I had something to prove. It was
as if I was trying to say, "Look at me, I am capable of
someone liking me and able to keep a man." Looking back,
I think of that mindset as simply pathetic. Why?

Not only have I changed my way of thinking, but also, I
changed the way I lived my life. I started seeking God
more, I started working out more (still have a weakness for

bread and pasta, but I'm working on it). I started journaling more, working on my brand, and overall just living life to the fullest. The things that bothered me then don't bother me anymore. I'm working hard to get to where I want to be in life. I forgot about the things that mattered to me, such as my modeling. Since my moving on, I have put all my energy into my passions.

God gave me the vision to write this very book. Never in a million years, did I think I would be writing a book. I held off because I didn't think that anyone would want to hear my story. I didn't want to put anyone on blast and I didn't want any problems. I was simply scared, until I prayed and received several confirmations that this is what I was supposed to be doing. I was reminded that you should never be afraid to tell your story. There is always someone willing to hear what you have been through. There is always someone that may be going through exactly what you have experienced. Transparency is key. I've always appreciated those surrounded by me that have been transparent and have told their story. If I have touched but only one person, then I have completed my mission in life.

Chapter 11:

Bouncing Back

"He said to them: 'It is not for you to know the times or dates the Father has set by his own authority." Acts 1:7

Bouncing Back to Me

*B*ouncing back requires me to stay focused on my mission and staying in my own lane. Before, I had a problem of comparing myself to others. I had a problem with being happy for other people. I had a problem when it seemed as if other people were making more progress than me, when I had been doing it longer. You want to know my biggest problem? I was so mad with God when it seemed like other people who I knew were living a wild and crazy life, were getting all the blessings, and here I was trying to live right and my career seemed to be at a stand still.

I was rushing God's progress. I wanted it on my own time. I had no time to wait. In my mind, I was thinking that models don't have much of a career after the age of 30, so I don't have much time because I'm already in my twenties. I would wake up and say to myself, "Ok God, this is the day where I will meet someone that will push my career to the next level!" I would go to sleep each night feeling disappointed because I didn't meet the mystery person. I had worked so hard and consistently that I felt as if I still wasn't enough. All I needed were connections. All I needed was for someone to recognize me and see that I was a great model, a great TV personality. I felt like no one noticed me. Sure, I was getting modeling gigs, but it felt as if I wasn't going any higher. I wasn't advancing.

One day I turned on the TV and the channel happened to be on the Trinity Broadcast Network (TBN). There was Pastor Joel Osteen talking about being faithful and patient for God's promises. He used the example of Sarah in the Bible not being patient for the child that God had promised her and her husband Abraham. Instead of waiting patiently, she gave permission to her husband to sleep with Hagar;

and together they birthed Ishmael. Now Ishmael was not the son that God promised Sarah and Abraham. God promised the son would come from Sarah, not Hagar. However, considering her old age, Sarah didn't see that as being possible. So she became impatient and decided to take things into her own hands.

That's how we as believers can sometimes be. That's how I was. We hear from God. We hear his promises and imagine ourselves living in the promise. Yet, many of us become impatient. At least that's how it was for me.

Pastor Osteen said, "Don't be out here birthing Ishmaels, when God wants to give you Isaac!"

I stopped in my tracks when I heard that. Just moments before, I was sitting in my car crying because I felt as if my dreams were never going to come true. I felt as if, my time had run out. I was too busy focused and concerned with what everyone else had going on in their life, that I forgot

about what God had promised me. I forgot about what he

had promised my family. I had forgot everything. I had to

bounce back and remember everything I was told. I had to

remember who I was. In that moment I had to wipe away

the tears and get back to my hustle. I had to go out and

make connections. Sometimes I can be really shy and

scared to talk to people that I know could help me reach the

next level, but I prayed and asked God to give me the

confidence that I was lacking. I needed confidence to be

bold and unafraid to meet new people. My sister would

always lecture me and tell me I couldn't be afraid to talk to

someone. She was right, as usual.

The Bible says in 1st Timothy chapter four and verse 14,

"Do not neglect your gift." I read that and it all hit me at

once. God gave me this gift, so why am I pouting about it

not happening fast enough? He's already ordained my pathway before I was born. He already knows what's instore for my future; I just have to trust Him and allow Him to guide me. Truth be told, if He would've given it to me when I was younger, there's no telling how I would be now. I probably would've been addicted to fame, acting out of character or just wild out here in these Hollywood streets. So, thank you God for not giving it to me when I truly was not ready.

Whatever you do, don't neglect your gift. Don't neglect your talents. You may not be in the place you want to be just yet, but trust and believe, if God has shown you, it will come to pass. God is not a man that he should lie.(Numbers 23:19) His words and promises always come true and they never fail. It could be 20 years from now, but it will happen. The current place that you are in is setting you up for your divine purpose. Even the people you don't think could help you in your destiny are a part of your purpose. Get out there, and make those connections.

I've always been told that I have a beautiful personality. Well I started putting it to good use. I was blessed to go to New Orleans for Essence Festival. Traci Evans, owner of Meow& Barks Boutique, invited my friends and me to model her clothes the entire weekend. It was an experience like no other. I met some really nice people and gained many connections. I left there thinking to myself wow, one day I'll be speaking here. One day I'll be on a billboard. One day, I will get to tell my story on a larger platform. One day, I'll be modeling for the designers I've always dreamed about. One day, I will reap the harvest God has promised my family and me.

Bouncing Back to Me

Everything I went through in my past was for a reason. It has made me the woman I am today. The things that I didn't know back then, set me up for what I know now and for the future. Everyone goes through heartbreak, setbacks and disappointments, but it's what you do after that. You can decide to lay in your mess, feel sorry for yourself or receive pity from other people. I choose to get up and try. I choose joy and love. I choose forgiveness. I choose to dust myself and try again (in the late singer Aaliyah's voice). I choose to trust God because He's the only person that is going to see me through.

Don't worry about which direction to take. Allow God to order your steps. Allow God to open those doors that no man can close. Allow God to show up and show out. Allow God to move into your life. If it wasn't for God, I have no clue where I would be. If it weren't for His grace and unearned favor, I would probably still be crying about my failed relationships. Still crying about how so and so hurt my feelings. Still crying about when things don't go my way.

Ever since God delivered me from a lot of things, I've always been terrified to speak my truth; to tell my testimony. But, no longer am I afraid. There are many people, especially women that have gone through or currently going though the same experiences. I now know the importance of being transparent. Whenever you feel that you are alone in something, understand that you are not. Before, I thought that no one cared about what I had going on. I felt that I couldn't talk to anyone about it, and for that, I kept it all bottled up inside. I was hurting so badly. I had deep issues within myself. I allowed the enemy to get into my mind during certain periods. Until I realized who I was and who my Father in Heaven is. I had to remind myself that I am a child of God and that the devil had no place in my mind.

During the time of my healing and transitioning to Tampa, I started writing scriptures on index cards and placing them on my bedroom wall next to my bed. I currently have close to 100 scriptures on my wall that I wake up to every morning. Sometimes I recite a few, depending on what I'm going through. Sometimes I just wake up and stare at all of them. For me, my wall of scriptures is a reminder of God's word. I'll hold my head up and my eyes will instantly look at the scripture I need to read. A friendly reminder of God telling me, "I got you. I'm not going anywhere." And I'm a witness to tell you; He's not going anywhere. He is omnipresent. Even when you feel like you're alone, he's right next to you. I've

Bouncing Back to Me

learned to just step aside and let God do what He does best: work it out for my good.

Bouncing back to me, took some time. I probably would've bounced back sooner if I had listened to the voice of God, my awesome parents and my sister sooner. Although it took a lot of time, I have no regrets. I am on a wonderful path towards the woman God has always purposed me to be. Will I make mistakes along the way? Most likely. Will I always have the right answer? No way. Will I need some help during my journey? Of course. I am not perfect nor do I claim to be. I simply want to be a better me. Being perfect is boring anyway. Before he passed away after his last sermon, the late Pastor Rudolph C. Mims told the church, "My past is my past." One day I remembered those same words in his voice. Those same words, helped me bounce back.

THE END

Acknowledgments

First off, THANK YOU JESUS! What would I do without
your grace and mercy? Thank you for never giving up on
me, even when I had given up on myself. Thank you for
being my peace. Thank you for pushing me into higher
heights and never failing me. The obstacles I went through
to be the woman I am today…whew! I never would have
made it without you.

Mommy and Daddy: You two have been my biggest
supporters throughout this process of mine called life.
When everyone else spoke their opinions of what I should
do with my life, you both supported what I wanted to do.
You have guided me in so many ways and gave me the best
gift of all, introducing me to Jesus. I will always be grateful
for that.

Tamara: My first role model growing up. I wanted to be
like you in so many ways. As I grow older I realize it was
okay to go my own path, knowing you'd still be the big

sister watching over me. Thank you for wiping the tears away when I needed you. I couldn't have asked for a better sister. You and Morris have been a wonderful example of marriage and I thank you both for the endless amount of men advice.

My Family: Way too many people to mention, but to my entire family, thank you for your continued support and love. I will forever be grateful. To my nephews, Terell, Moe, Joshua, Miles and Noah…I hope to be the aunty you always call on if you need a break from your parents…the cool aunt.

Uncle Gary: Thank you for funding this book. You have always been there for the family, especially for my mother. You are the O.G. I didn't want to bother you, but thank you for always having my back. As always, you pulled through!

BGM: Taylor, Brielle, Ty'ra, Allana…. simply I love you all. My adult years so far have been LIT because of our friendship. You all push me to do better. You all are the greatest friends I could ask for. Sometimes we annoy each other, but that's what sisters do.

Evangelist/Author Amikco N. Marolt and Ninon Rhome: My awesome editors! I thank you both for editing and guiding me through this process. You two have been huge influencers on my life. I was just a young woman with a dream to write a book and the both of you helped make it possible!

Bishop and First Lady Maxwell: International Harvest Church of God stand up! I love my church! Thank you Bishop and First Lady Maxwell for being my covering since moving to Tampa. I have grown so much spiritually being under your leadership. Thank you both for leading by example. Thank you to all IHC members that have helped me and prayed for me along the way.

My Tampa Family: I always tell people, I was born and raised in Jacksonville, FL, but Tampa is where I became a woman. The people I have met since being here and the lessons I've learned are mind blowing! My roommates, Phoebe and Samantha, the Gospel Choir at USF, Lafayette, Britany, Tim, Deja, Wes, Kat my coworkers, my brothers of Alpha Phi Omega (especially my big, Xan, and my little, Yaya), my neighbors, etc., I love you all so much. Thank you for being my home away from home.

LaTavia: Girl it's so scary how we are walking a similar path. Every time I talk to you, its like we are living the same lives or going through the exact situation. Thank you for being my prayer partner. You are more than just my makeup artist. You are my sister. I love you.

Thank you to everyone that has ever sown a seed into my life, helped in any way with my modeling career, prayed for me, taught me, etc. Your support does not go unnoticed.

Until next time…

Thank you all for reading.

Made in the USA
Columbia, SC
05 October 2018